50 Table Topics

by Wang C. Yip

Contents

CHAPTER ONE

Chapter 1: Why Table Topics?

What will you get out of this book?

Being a Toastmaster for 8 years, I firmly believe that table topics is the one aspect of a Toastmaster meeting that has the opportunity to turn a good meeting into a great meeting. It can be a way to create laughter, challenge members and let guests see how fun a club can be.

During my time as a Toastmaster, I have always taken an innovative and creative approach to table topics that have consistently surprised members (in a good way) and attracted guests to come back to another meeting to learn more about Toastmasters (or better yet, join the club). I want to share some of the table topic ideas that I believe are some of the best ideas that I have seen and used at Toastmaster meetings. I will provide the idea, sample prompts that you can use, the general logistics for executing the idea in the right way and why the idea is great.

Note that this book does not cover things like the format, timing or structure of a good table topic. You can find this information online in a variety of sources.

What are table topics?

Table topics are a part of every Toastmaster meeting. For more information on what Toastmasters is, google Toastmasters.

Table topics are prompts, usually inspired by the meeting theme but not always, and members and guests are asked to provide their thoughts on the prompts in a short speech. Table topics are incredibly useful because everybody uses these skills but rarely have the chance to practice or refine them. We use impromptu speaking when we go to job interviews, dates, networking events, elevator pitches and we never know when we will get asked questions that we need to be ready for.

What are the different skills that you use when practicing table topics?

- *Listening effectively-* You have to make sure that you are answering the right question before you answer the question right.

- *Being concise* - Usually, table topics are a maximum of two minutes and therefore, you have to be able to get your point across in a concise and effective manner.

- *Understanding the speech structure* - Even in a short speech, having a structure can not only help you deliver your speech, but it will also help your audience understand and remember your speech.

- *Gauging the audience's reaction* - Sometimes you can see how the audience is reacting to the different things in your speech and then change your speech on the fly.

- *Taking a side or forming a quick opinion* - You do not have a lot of time to think about your speech and you have to be able to take a side or form a quick opinion and then expand on it as you deliver your speech. This is the case, even if you do not like either side of the fence.

- *Pivoting or reframing* - Sometimes you receive a question that you do not know how to answer or have a good answer for and therefore, pivoting to another topic or reframing the topic so that you can answer it in a different way.

Using table topics as icebreakers or team building exercises

Although I have framed these ideas as table topics for toastmaster meetings, you can also use these ideas to help break the ice for group sessions or as team building exercises for board retreats or orientations. Please note that not all of the ideas will work because some ideas will require equipment or a certain amount of space, but feel free to be creative!

CHAPTER TWO

Chapter 2: Table Topic Ideas

Scents and Memories

Idea:

Partly inspired by an episode of House and partly inspired by my biology professor who talked about how the more senses that were engaged, the more you could remember, this table topic idea is based on the fact that certain smells can bring about incredibly intense and vivid memories.

Equipment needed:

Please bring items or ingredients that have distinct smells to the meeting.

What the audience needs to know:

Please ask the audience if they have any allergic reactions. If they do, I recommend eliminating certain items under the sample prompts.

Logistics:

Table topic speakers will come to the front of the room and be blindfolded. They will be given a whiff of something with a distinct smell. They are to share with the audience the first thing that comes to their mind when they smell the item. It is also important that they are blindfolded so that they do not see the item and have any pre-determined thoughts or ideas in their head.

Sample prompts:

- Rubbing alcohol
- Cinnamon (or any spice in your cupboard that has a distinct smell - I recommend pouring a small amount out into a zip lock bag rather than bringing the whole spice shaker)
- Shoe polish
- Fruits

- Peppermint
- Chocolate
- Vanilla
- Any scented soap
- Dryer sheet

Please remember to ask if any Toastmaster members have allergies before conducting table topics.

Why this idea is great:

This idea, with a small amount of preparation can create speeches that can be on any topic. You certainly do not need to follow the theme of the meeting, but this table topic can be used for a wide variety of different themes including aromas, memories, nostalgia or really any seasonal or event themed meeting.

Positive Spin

Idea:

I used to work at UBC as an Orientations Coordinator and as part of our responsibilities, we volunteered to do summer tours for prospective students. One of my friends, also an Orientations Coordinator, did a tour and told us that one of the students asked her about all the construction that was happening on campus. Generally, construction is not seen in a positive light due to the constant rerouting of students around main paths; however, when asked about the construction, my friend said that "UBC is constantly renovating and improving". It was a fantastic way of spinning what is typically seen as a nuisance into something positive. This is the main idea for this table topic.

Equipment needed:

No equipment needed.

What the audience needs to know:

The table topic idea will be similar to other ideas. A topic will be chosen and an audience member will be chosen at random to speak on the topic. That topic will be something negative, but the table topic speaker's responsibility is to spin that negative topic into something positive.

Logistics:

Provide the prompt and then ask a table topic speaker to come to the front of the room to speak on the topic.

Sample prompts:

- You are the mayor of a town that has just been destroyed by Godzilla - why is that a good thing?
- You are the owner of a business that has just gone bankrupt - why is this great?
- You have just been divorced - why is this fantastic?
- You have just been fired from your job but you are happier than ever - why?
- You just went to the doctor and found out that you only have 1 year to live - why is this good?
- Due to a freak accident, your home has burned down and you do not have any insurance so you are now homeless - why is this good?
- Fantasy scenario: due to crazy science experiments conducted, you are trapped in a house surrounded by zombies - why is this good?

Other 'bad luck' scenarios can be added as appropriate.

Why this idea is great:

There can be quite a bit of pessimism in the world and this table topic idea can help to inject a bit of optimism into the meeting and the members. It can also be a great way of injecting some creativity and some humour into the meeting because often times, by forcing people to be optimistic and reframing different scenarios, they can bring to light different things that others may not have thought of before. This table topic also does not require a great deal of preparation other than preparing the different 'bad luck' scenarios so it can be used on a whim when someone has to step in as a table topics master at the last minute.

Action replay

Idea:

The first table topic speaker will perform a scene with exaggerated physical movements while the second table topic speaker will observe visually but not hear the dialogue of the table topic speaker performing the scene. The second table topic speaker will then re-enact the same motions and develop a new table topic based on the same motions performed by the first table topic speaker. This is then repeated: the first table topic speaker will perform a scene with exaggerated physical movements while the second table topic speaker will perform the same scene with the same motions but with a different table topic.

Equipment needed:

Please bring headphones (the ones that go over the ears), a smartphone or music player to the meeting.

What the audience needs to know:

The first table topic speaker will need to perform a scene with exaggerated physical movements. The crazier the actions, the better.

The audience, especially the second table topic speaker, will need to pay close attention to the first table topic speaker and their body language / movements as they perform the table topic. They do not necessarily need to repeat the same actions in the same order as it may be quite difficult to remember all the different actions, but it does provide the table topic speaker with more material to develop a table topic speech.

Logistics:

After explaining table topics, the table topic master will choose the second table topic speaker first and ask him / her to put on headphones so that they cannot hear what the first table topic speaker says. The table topic master will then choose a topic (one that is very visual and can be enhanced by a lot of actions) and then ask someone from the audience to perform that table topic.

After the first table topic, the second table topic speaker will take off his headphones and perform the same actions but with a different topic. If the table topic master wishes to make it more challenging for the second table topic speaker, they can ask the audience for a subject or choose a theme themselves for the table topic speech.

Sample prompts:

- Describe your favourite sports and why you like the sports so much
- Describe your childhood, what did you like to do and why?
- Tell us about the last time you went to a playground, what did you do?

- Tell us the last time you made a decision that you regretted - what did you do?
- You work as a carpenter and you have to construct your own home - what would you put in your house and why?
- Imagine that you are Indiana Jones, tell us about your latest adventure
- Have you ever gotten lost in a forest - what happened and how did you find your way out?
- Where is your favourite place outdoors? What do you like to do?
- Tell us about your favourite exercises in the gym

Why this idea is great:

This idea requires little preparation but can be a lot of fun because it really focuses on body language and how we use it to emphasize our speeches. Not only that, but it is possible to have a completely different speech even if you have the same body language in two speeches. A great way to inspire creativity is to construct an artificial 'box' of rules to see how people adapt to it. In this case, the box is the body movement as the table topic speaker has to use the same actions, but create a completely new table topic speech based on those actions. People will laugh at how crazy the body language is but also how creative the table topic speakers will be in 'justifying' the actions that they're talking about.

Bring a book

Idea:

I love reading and of course I also love books. This is a great table topic idea if your members love reading and they want to be exposed to new books. For this table topic (and it also works great as a meeting theme), everybody brings their favourite book or a book that they are currently reading. The table topics master will mix up the books and then choose one book for a table topic speaker to speak on.

Equipment needed:

All members will bring their favourite book or a book that they are currently reading. Guests may also join the meeting and therefore it is important to bring a few extra books so that guests are not left out.

What the audience needs to know:

Before the meeting, all members are required to bring a book of their choosing to the meeting. It must be a printed copy, but it can also be a newspaper or magazine.

Logistics:

The table topic master will collect all the books at the front of the room. They will then randomly choose a book, introduce the book title and then choose a table topic speaker to provide a book review and tell the audience why they recommend the book to others in the audience.

Another way that the table topics master can provide topics is by introducing the book title and then reading a small passage or quote from the book. They can then choose a table topic speaker to talk about what that quote means to them and why they would recommend the book to others.

Sample prompts:

None - prompts are based on the books provided.

Why this idea is great:

Who doesn't like learning? Books can be a fantastic way of learning from others (hey, aren't you reading a book now?) and it's not just learning from others, but learning from others in a compressed time frame. Why learn in a few years when you can learn from a book that has distilled that same knowledge into a readable form? Plus, you can learn a lot about other members from the books that they read and what they are interested in.

Unknown job interview

Idea:

I always enjoy when we have table topics that allow the audience to be a part of an inside joke (see **Press Conference** or **Action replay** for similar 'inside joke' type table topics). In this case, I always thought about how table topics was a good way of preparing you for job interviews but I have not seen any table topics where we actually conduct interviews. I thought I would do mock interviews, but add in a twist.

Equipment needed:

Please bring headphones (the ones that go over the ears), a smartphone or music player to the meeting.

What the audience needs to know:

If an audience member is selected as the 'job applicant', they will be required to answer honestly and answer questions without knowing what they are interviewing for (i.e., they will make up answers). If an audience member is selected as the 'interviewer', they will conduct an interview with the job applicant as they see fit. They will ask more general questions near the beginning. As time runs out for the table topic speech, they will ask more specific questions that hint to what job the applicant is interviewing for.

Logistics:

The table topic master will select a table topic speaker. That table topic speaker will put on headphones and will be the job applicant. Another audience member will be chosen as the job interviewer and be told what job they will be interviewing the table topic speaker for.

Tips for the job interviewer:
- Keep the questions flowing
- Keep the questions generic at the beginning and more specific near the end (i.e., questions that hint at what job the applicant is interviewing for)

Sample prompts:

Here are a few sample questions:

General questions (to be asked near the beginning of the job interview)
- What interests you in this job?
- What interests you about this company?
- Why should we hire you over another job candidate?
- What special skills do you think you can bring to this job?
- Tell me what relevant experience do you bring to this job?
- Where do you see this industry going in the future?

Why this idea is great:

This is a fantastic way of both preparing for job interviews and being aware of how you might come across as an interviewer. Interviewing others is an invaluable skill for those that are moving up in their companies or will be eventually moving up into management. As an interviewer, you will learn how to ask questions, how to elicit answers from someone that is nervous and how to build rapport and calm the nerves of a potential candidate that you are trying to assess.

Children's pictures

Idea:

As I was browsing the Internet, I found some children's pictures that I thought would make great table topics because of the way it might be interpreted by adults. Children have such a fresh perspective on things that I thought it would be interesting to see what members would think.

Equipment needed:

The table topics master will print out various pictures before the meeting from the sample prompts below. If the club has access to a projector, they can download the pictures and present them on the screen.

What the audience needs to know:

Each table topic speaker will be provided a picture at random and will be asked to interpret what the child was thinking when they drew the picture.

Logistics:

The table topic master will select a picture at random, show the picture to the audience and then select a table topic speaker to speak on that picture. Each table topic speaker will be asked to take on the role of parent and asked to describe what their child was thinking when they drew that picture.

Sample prompts:

Google "hilarious children's pictures" for a few prompts

http://www.dailymail.co.uk/femail/article-3033690/The-hilarious-children-s-drawings-definitely-did-NOT-make-family-fridge.html

http://www.rantlifestyle.com/2015/01/20/17-accidentally-hilarious-childrens-drawings/

http://www.thebestpageintheuniverse.net/c.cgi?u=irule

Why this idea is great:

A picture can mean a thousand words (which is a little too much for a table topic speech given the rate of speech is about 120 words a minute and that a table topic speech is usually a maximum of 2 minutes) but often times, the pictures, through the filter of an adult, can be interpreted in different ways when the true meaning of the picture can be completely innocent.

Secret fact

Idea:

Everyone will write down a secret fact and the table topic speeches will be guesses as to who wrote that fact and why they think so.

Equipment needed:

- Ballots
- Pens / pencils

What the audience needs to know:

Everyone will take a ballot and write down a secret fact that very few people know about them. If they are not comfortable writing down a secret fact about themselves, they can write down a random fact. The table topic master will announce a fact and choose a table topic speaker to talk about that fact. Each table topic speaker will try to identify who wrote the fact and why they think it is that person. For example, the fact might be "Loves playing violin" and you think Jack wrote this fact because he is always humming and he has quick hands.

Logistics:

The table topic master will ask everyone in the audience (including guests) to write down a secret fact that very few people know about them. It helps save time if they announce this at the beginning and then explain what table topics is, the timing, the structure for table topics and the fact that everyone will vote on their favourite table topic speaker as the audience is writing down a secret fact. After the audience has written down a fact, the table topic master will collect the ballots and then randomly draw one fact. After announcing the fact, they will ask "who do you think wrote this" and then announce the table topic speaker.

Sample prompts:

- None, the audience will write down facts.

Why this idea is great:

This is a great table topic idea to use because not a lot of preparation is needed beforehand and the members get to learn something new about each other. Often times, the members will learn something new about a guest or a member and that helps to create conversations either during the break or after the meeting (especially if guest facts are chosen).

Evil challenges

Idea:

A lot of these challenges were inspired by some of the interesting challenges and quirks in improv games. I introduced these challenges as part of table topics and found that it did something that a lot of table topics didn't do with many of the senior members: it made them take pause to think about the table topic and it was both challenging and fun.

Equipment needed:

None.

What the audience needs to know:

Table topics will proceed just like any other regular table topics session except that each table topic speaker will be given a challenge that they will have to perform during the table topic speech.

Logistics:

The table topics master will prepare a list of challenges beforehand randomly numbered. The table topics master will then provide the same table topic speech to everyone in the audience. Once the table topics master has selected a speaker, they will ask the speaker for a number and that will identify the challenge that the table topics speaker will have to perform during their table topic speech.

Sample prompts:

Any table topic question can be used, however these are some challenges that you can provide them as table topic master:

- Change consonant (pick a consonant and change that with another consonant. For example, all m's become p's so when they say Toastmaster, they should be saying Toastpaster")
- Only 5 word sentences (all sentences that the table topics speaker uses will consist of 5 words)
- Chain sentences (all sentences begin with the last letter of the last sentence they used. For example "Fellow Toastmasters and most welcome guests. Some would say that summer only lasts a few months in Edmonton. Not me. Easy to say that since I really enjoy the winters. Somebody told me that there are three seasons in Edmonton: summer, winter and construction. Normally, I would laugh but I entirely agree."
- 1 -> 5 -> 1 sentences (sentences consist of one word, then two words, then three, all the way to five and then back down to one word sentences)
- Word of the day (use the word of the day 5 times. If the club does not have a word of the day, the table topics master can choose a word that is rarely used instead)
- Movement around the room (the table topics speaker is required to walk around the room at

least 2 times in a natural way)
- Alphabet sentences (every sentence begins with the next letter of the alphabet, starting at "A". For example: "A llama wanted to eat me. Bolting away was the only thing that saved me. Can I get some applause?"
- Questions only (the table topic speaker can only speak in questions)

Feel free to add different challenges or change up the challenges in a variety of ways (e.g., use only 4 word sentences OR change consonant can be used multiple times).

Why this idea is great:

While everyone is provided the table topics question at the very beginning of the table topics session, the challenges thrown in really throw off table topics speakers. This does not require a lot of preparation and can really challenge table topics speakers.

PowerPoint karaoke

Idea:

Have you ever been to a business presentation where the presenter brought up the wrong PowerPoint deck and then tried to talk their way through it? No? Well it could happen! That's where this idea came from. All table topic speakers will walk the audience through a PowerPoint deck on a subject that is pre-determined by the audience. This is a lot of fun, especially when the slides are randomly chosen images.

Equipment needed:

- Projector
- Computer
- PowerPoint
- Stock images (from pixabay, pexels, death to stock photos and other sources)

What the audience needs to know:

The table topic speaker will come in front of the room. The table topic master will ask the audience for a random topic that they would hear at a leadership conference. It could be "synergy" or "time management". The slides will be changed by the table topics master.

Logistics:

Before the meeting, the table topic master should prepare about 10 PowerPoint decks with 8 random images (all different) in each of the decks. The title page could be "Table Topic Speech #1", "Table Topic Speech #2", etc. and then there would be the 8 images.

The table topics master will introduce the table topic speaker with the random topic and then will control the PowerPoint deck. As the table topic speaker finishes a paragraph or gets stuck on the subject, the table topic master can switch the slides. Depending on the number of slides, the table topic master will have to switch the slides accordingly (e.g., with 8 slides and a 2 minute time limit for the table topic speech, each slide will be on for 15 seconds).

Sample prompts:

- Search for different images that have something tangible in them. Order does not matter but if you want to make it easier on Table Topic Speakers, you can arrange them around a particular theme like "Adventure" or "Love".

Why this idea is great:

Table topic speakers will be challenged with this table topic, but if they ever get stuck, they can look to the images and get ideas on what to talk on next. Table topic speakers will still need to have an opening, body and conclusion and the audience will find it funny when the images are extremely different from what the speaker is talking about or if the images coincidentally match what the speaker is talking about.

Press Conference

Idea:

Think of a press conference where an athlete is announcing his retirement or a President is announcing a big change in policy. There's a short announcement and then he / she fields questions from the audience about the subject. In this table topic idea, each table topic speaker will do a press conference where they do not know what they have just announced and they have to guess based on the audience's questions.

Equipment needed:

Please bring headphones (the ones that go over the ears), a smartphone or music player to the meeting.

What the audience needs to know:

The audience needs to understand that as they ask questions, they will slowly drop hints as to what the table topic speaker announced. The first few questions will be generic, but the audience will have to pay attention to the timing and provide more pointed questions as the table topic speech goes along.

The table topic speaker will be making up answers as they go along and as the audience drops hints through the questions, they will guess what the announcement was at the end of the table topic.

Logistics:

The table topic speaker will come to the front of the room and put on the headphones with loud music playing so that he / she cannot hear the prompt. As table topics master, you will choose a prompt for the table topic speaker to act out. Since the table topic speaker has headphones on, everyone except the table topic speaker knows what he / she is announcing. Once you have announced the prompt, ask the table topic speaker to go to the front of the room and begin fielding questions. The onus is on the audience to continue asking questions until the time runs out OR the table topic speaker knows the announcement that they have just 'made'.

Sample prompts:

- Santa Claus retiring
- The Queen of England visiting your city
- First Astronaut to make love in space
- Batman coming out of the closet
- Just won a lifetime supply of X (choose a strange meal)
- Tin Man having a child with Dorothy
- Noah announces he has eaten all the animals on the ark
- Has lived 6 months in a whale

- Head transplanted to a dog's body

Why this idea is great:

This idea is one of, if not the best, ideas I have ever used in my Toastmaster career. Every club and member that I conduct this table topic on has loved the idea and it is great for so many reasons: it is fun, it is challenging, it engages the audience, it engages the guests without pressuring them to speak in front of the group and lastly, right when the prompt is revealed, the audience has an 'inside joke' that they have with each other.

Unanswerable questions

Idea:

There is a huge list of unanswerable questions that will really make Toastmaster members think and at the same time make them laugh.

Equipment needed:

A list of questions is all that is needed.

What the audience needs to know:

Each table topic speaker will come to the front of the room and be asked to provide an opinion or explanation on the question asked.

Logistics:

Provide the prompt first and then ask a table topic speaker to come to the front of the room to speak on the topic.

Sample prompts:

- If a bunch of cats jump on top of each other, is it still called a dog pile?
- If a doctor suddenly had a heart attack while doing surgery, would the other doctors work on the doctor or the patient?
- Why does caregiver and caretaker mean the same thing?
- If you had a three story house and were in the second floor, isn't it possible that you can be upstairs and downstairs at the same time?
- If quitters never win, why do they tell us to quit while we're ahead?
- When French people swear, do they say "pardon my English?"
- Do coffins have lifetime guarantees?
- If it's zero degrees outside today and it's supposed to be twice as cold tomorrow, how cold is it going to be?
- How fast do hotcakes sell?
- Why do doctors call what they do practice?
- Why do fat chance and slim chance mean the same thing?
- If your clone kills you, is that suicide?
- If vegetarians love animals so much, why do they eat all their food?
- How do you tell when you run out of invisible ink?
- How come wrong numbers are never busy?

More can be found by searching for Crazy Thoughts or unanswerable questions on google.

Why this idea is great:

I always like table topics that throw in a random question because often times, even the best Toastmasters are slightly stumped given that there is no right answer and no immediately obvious logical answer to the question. This table topic is a table topic that speakers have to work their way through and then build a conclusion off of the things that they have talked about as opposed to forming a conclusion right away and justifying your conclusion through your ideas (i.e., what good table topic speakers normally do). It can be uncomfortable working in this way but it can also be immensely rewarding to come to a conclusion that makes sense even after trying to ramble your way through the table topic speech.

Moving people

Idea:

With this table topic, I wanted to explore what happens when body language, which plays such a vital role in communications, is not used when speaking. This table topic is inspired by the improv game of the same name called "moving people".

Equipment needed:

None.

What the audience needs to know:

Two table topics speakers will be chosen to speak on a particular situation; however, they are not allowed to move their bodies at all. Two more audience members will be chosen to move the bodies of the two table topic speakers in any way they choose (but not in any inappropriate ways). As the table topics speakers speak, the two volunteers will move the table topics speakers in various ways to adapt to the situation or whatever they think is logical.

Logistics:

Two table topics speakers will act out a situation chosen by the table topics master. The table topics master will ask the two table topics speakers not to move at all. Two additional volunteers will be chosen from the audience to move the two table topics speakers. Once the two volunteers have moved the bodies of the table topics speakers, the table topics speakers will stay in that position until moved again.

Sample prompts:

- Two hikers are lost in the mountains and trying to find their way home
- C3PO and R2D2 are trying to find Luke Skywalker
- A coach is trying to help his basketball player during half time
- A teacher is tutoring a student through a difficult math problem
- Two pirates are trying to decide how to divide up the treasure loot

Why this idea is great:

It can feel weird not having control of your body while speaking and this table topic will definitely make table topics speakers aware of how much they might rely or depend on their body language in order to emphasize different messages or pass along messages to the audience in subtle ways. Since the volunteers are moving the bodies, they will not react as quickly as if the table topics speakers moved themselves so it can be quite funny when the table topics speakers are describing what is happening to their body or adapting their table topic speeches based on what is or is not happening with their body language.

Sentences

Idea:

This is based on a fun improv game I saw on Whose Line is it Anyway. In the game, the two performers are handed different slips of paper with random sentences on them. They are asked to perform a scene and at various moments throughout the scene, they take out a slip of paper and read out the sentence (not having read the sentences beforehand). After saying the sentences out loud, they will then have to incorporate the sentences into the scene in an appropriate way.

Equipment needed:

None, although preparing slips of paper with random sentences beforehand could be one way to prepare.

What the audience needs to know:

The audience will all be asked the same table topic question (or for a more challenging variation, you can perform a regular session of table topics with the slips of paper as an extra challenge) and when the table topic hits the green light, they have to read out the slip of paper and incorporate the random sentence into their speech in some way. They are not supposed to read the sentence beforehand as it will be a lot more fun when they read it and try to incorporate it into whatever they were just talking about, but there are no hard rules.

Logistics:

The main way that I like to conduct this table topic is to announce the table topic question to everyone at the very beginning of table topics and state that everyone will be answering the same table topic question. The table topic master will then ask everyone to rip off a slip of paper, either off of their ballots or off of a piece of scrap paper and to write down a random statement or question. After gathering all the statements, the table topic master will then ask one person to give a table topic speech and hand them a randomly selected slip of paper.

Other variations include one or more of the following:
- preparing the random statements ahead of time
- asking everyone different table topic questions
- having two table topic speakers perform a scene

Sample prompts:

You can either have everyone in the audience write down something or prepare prompts ahead of time.

- I like big butts and I cannot lie.
- Who wants sausages and sauerkraut?
- The chicken dance is the official dance of the Olympics.

- Is it me you're waiting for?
- Frogs are cool animals.
- I stepped on a corn flake and now I'm a cereal killer.
- I'm so blue, I'm greener than purple.

Other sentences can be found by googling "random sentences".

Why this idea is great:

It does not require a lot of preparation and adds a lot of fun and laughter into a meeting without any extra effort. I think a lot of people think that humour is forced sometimes and with this table topic, they can see that just the juxtaposition of a table topic speech and a random sentence can be entertaining and get laughs in more ways than one.

Quirky characteristics

Idea:

I enjoy themes (and table topics) in which people act out of their comfort zone within the safety of the Toastmasters club. Of course, this requires a club who is also okay acting quirky or different for one meeting. Everybody is given a quirk or characteristic that they will have to act out during table topics (or it can be expanded to the meeting itself) and they have to answer the table topic with that quirk or characteristic in mind.

Equipment needed:

None but slips of paper with quirks or characteristics should be prepared beforehand.

What the audience needs to know:

Each audience member will be provided with a slip of paper with a quirk or characteristic that they will act out for the duration of table topics. For example, someone might be given a slip of paper that reads "easily irritated" and when answering a table topic question, they might vent a story of frustration at something quite trivial.

Logistics:

Once table topics starts, the table topics master will hand out a quirk / characteristic to everyone and ask them to incorporate that characteristic into their table topic speech. They should not reveal the characteristic to others. At the end of table topics (or the meeting), the audience members can guess what everyone's characteristic was.

Sample prompts:

- Easily irritated
- Loves animals
- Short attention span
- Talks more with their hands than with their mouth
- Extremely active - always working out
- Talks in third person
- Thinks the Toastmaster is extremely attractive
- Extremely charismatic
- Insults everyone
- Bursts into song at random
- Uses the word of the day in the wrong context

Why this idea is great:

This idea is great both as a table topic and a meeting theme. It can also be quite fun to see people acting uncharacteristically and then trying to guess what quirk or characteristic they are acting out.

Actor's nightmare

Idea:

Imagine an audition where actors have to say their lines while having someone else (like a director) read off of their script. I thought this would be an interesting way of being creative and reacting and incorporating dialogue that is not necessarily related to the scene.

Equipment needed:

Print outs of plays or movie scripts.

What the audience needs to know:

Table topics will consist of two table topics speakers who will perform a scene outlined by the table topics master. One table topic speaker will have a script and they can only read and say lines off of the script, nothing else. The other table topic speaker is free to say anything they want.

Logistics:

The table topics master will choose two table topic speakers. One table topic speaker will be able to speak freely while the other table topic speaker will be given a script. In order to provide everyone with equal speaking opportunity, it would be better to give the script to someone that already has a speaking role such as a Speech Evaluator or a General Evaluator. The table topic master will then outline the scene that the two table topics speakers will be performing.

Sample prompts:

- Two shoppers are siblings and looking for something to purchase for their parent's 50th anniversary
- Two adventurers are lost in the jungle and are trying to find their way back home.
- Two competing athletes are training for the Olympics.
- Two people are in a life coaching relationship (the coach is the one with the script while the person being coached can say anything they want).
- Two people are trying to decide what to eat for dinner.

Good prompts consist of outlining enough information for the table topics speakers to create a scene from but not so much information that the whole scene has been described to the smallest detail.

For a list of scripts to use, you can google "free monologues" and print out a few of them for your table topic speakers to read off of.

Why this idea is great:

Similar to the Sentences table topic idea, this requires the freely talking table topic speaker to react, adapt and incorporate the random sentences that the other table topic speaker is saying. At the same time, because the other table topic speaker is forced to speak only off of their script, they can also be creative in their answers or if they do not wish to think at all, they can just read random sentences even if they do not fit the scene or dialogue, although it will help the scene a lot more if it did fit.

Two headed expert

Idea:

Have you ever had to lie or back your friend up but were not sure what you had to lie about or how to back your friend. For instance, let's say you are a guy and you and your best friend recently had an epic night of partying. The morning after, your best friend's girlfriend calls to ask where her boyfriend is - what do you say? If you are a good 'bro', you might say that he is with you but is unable to speak right now even though you may not know why his girlfriend is calling. This table topic idea tries to capture that synchronicity between random Toastmasters.

Equipment needed:

None.

What the audience needs to know:

Table topics will consist of two table topic speakers coming up to the front of the room and being an 'expert' in a topic selected by the table topics master. The table topics master will then quiz them on the subject. The trick is that the expert is actually a two headed person and they can only speak one word at a time.

Logistics:

Two table topic speakers are selected and for the purposes of table topics, they are now an expert on a topic selected by the table topics master. They will have to answer every question they are given one word at a time.

For a more challenging variation, the two headed expert will now speak at the same time rather than one word at a time (i.e., they have to come up with the same words at the same time). This will require the two table topics speakers to watch each other closely and to strike a balance between following what the other person is saying and leading the statements.

Sample prompts:

- Olympic gold for belching
- Architect of the Eiffel Tower
- Laziest person on earth
- Designer of the Pyramids
- Operations and maintenance for the Great Wall of China
- Longest streak for playing video games
- World record for hiccups
- Has hitchhiked across the world

Note that experts do not actually have to be experts in the subject matter chosen but it can certainly help. All answers and questions can be made up.

Why this idea is great:

This table topic is a great way to learn how to read body language and react to the cues of someone that you might not know very well. Again, it is another easy way to add humour and entertainment to a meeting without having to prepare jokes or set up long elaborate punchlines.

Backwards interview

Idea:

I love backwards meetings and therefore, this table topic idea, which is essentially a smaller version of the backwards meeting really appeals to me. The interview is conducted backwards (i.e., the first sentence spoken would be the last sentence of the interview, the second sentence spoken would be the second last sentence of the interview and so on).

Equipment needed:

None.

What the audience needs to know:

Two table topics speakers will be selected, one will be the interviewer and the other will be the interviewee. The interview will be conducted backwards. Careful attention must be paid by the table topics speakers as to what was just said as their response may be dependent on what was just said. For example "Thank you for your candid response." "Oh and I have a bad habit of sleeping in."

Logistics:

Two table topics speakers will be selected and one speaker will be the interviewer and the other will be the interviewee. The job that the interviewee is applying for will be selected at random by the table topics master or the audience. The scene begins with a handshake and any kind of statement at the end of the interview (e.g., "Thank you for coming in for this interview. I'll be in touch in 2 weeks to let you know our final decision. Thanks again."). The timing can be extended slightly to 2 - 3 minutes but personally, I would not want to extend it too long because this is something different and it might be difficult to keep the interview going in this new format.

Other variations can include two people in different scenes (not necessarily in a job interview).

Sample prompts:

Sample jobs that the interview could be for:
- Nurse
- Doctor
- Management consultant
- Couch tester
- Life guard
- Stay at home mom / dad
- IT analyst

Why this idea is great:

As I mentioned, I really like the backwards meeting format because it gets people out of their comfort zone and really forces them to think about the 'ending' and how to get to that ending. This is a great table topic because it really forces table topics speakers to listen to one another for cues on what they should be saying next. It can also be fun to see what questions the interviewer comes up with based on the answers that the interviewee gives.

Last line

Idea:

A lot of people think that creativity is free-form and unbounded, but often times we get creative when we are limited or bounded by different rules.

Equipment needed:

None.

What the audience needs to know:

Regular table topics questions will be asked; however, the trick is that the table topic speech must end with the line given by the table topics master. This means that the audience will have to work backwards from that line to develop a coherent speech that leads to that line. There are a variety of ways the line at the end of the speech can be incorporated but one example to give the audience could be "and then my friend said something random to me that I will never forget. She said <line>".

Logistics:

The table topics master will choose the topic and then provide the last line that is to be used for the table topic speech and then finally select a table topics speaker.

For example: "Our next table topic speaker will answer the question, what is the worst decision you've made in the past year and the last line will be 'Wednesday is hump day, but has anyone asked the camel if he's happy about it?' Bob, I want you to answer this one".

It may make sense to write down the last lines for table topics speakers to look at for their table topics speech.

Sample prompts:

You can use regular table topics questions but use the following sentences as last lines (or first lines).

- And that's why I'm never going back to Disneyland
- The moral of the story: buy high, sell low.
- War, what is it good for?
- It's money in the bank baby!
- It was gross but I kind of liked it.
- My Mum tries to be cool by saying that she likes all the same things that I do.
- Last Friday in three weeks' time I saw a spotted striped blue worm shake hands with a legless lizard.
- Wednesday is hump day, but has anyone asked the camel if he's happy about it?

- Lets all be unique together until we realise we are all the same.
- If you like tuna and tomato sauce- try combining the two. It's really not as bad as it sounds.
- I want to buy an onesie... but know it won't suit me.

The table topics master can also ask the audience to provide a random line that the table topics speech will have to end with.

Another variation could be providing table topics speakers with a first line and a last line that they have to use for their table topic speech.

Why this idea is great:

I enjoy being creative with my table topics, unfortunately, this also means that some of the really good ideas that I come up with are ones that I cannot participate in because I am the one conducting table topics. This table topic gives the table topics master a chance to be creative, showcase some humour and to develop a table topics master vs. the audience mentality where the table topics speakers try to stump the table topics master.

Silent auction

Idea:

One challenge that the club has, even though Toastmasters (and the clubs) are not-for-profit, is that money can be a concern, especially when trying to purchase invaluable things like lecterns, banner stands, prizes for contests, etc. This table topic can be a great way of exchanging goods between members for the benefit of the club.

Equipment needed:

Silent auction printouts with a blank space for the donator, the market price for the item, the minimum increment for the next bid, as well as a table for silent auction bid entries.

What the audience needs to know:

Members will be asked a week ahead of time to bring books, alcohol, gift baskets, gift cards, etc. All proceeds will go to the club. The meeting will have two breaks instead of the one break for a normal meeting and during those two breaks, members will be allowed to bid on any items they wish.

For table topics, the table topics master will randomly select one item from the lot and ask a member to recommend the item to the other members of the club.

Logistics:

A week before the meeting, all members should be informed that the next meeting will be a silent auction meeting and if they attend, should bring an item of their choice in good condition to donate to the silent auction. All proceeds will go to the club.

The meeting will have two table topic session rounds. Each table topic session round will be followed by a short break where members can bid on any of the items through the silent auction bid sheet. At the end of the second break, the bidding will be closed.

Sample prompts:

- Why is this item such a great purchase?
- Who do you think should purchase this item?
- How much money do you think this item is worth?
- What are the fringe benefits of owning this item (e.g., a book can also be a door stopper)

Why this idea is great:

Not only is this a different table topics session, it can also be a great way for boost the club and let members be charitable in giving items that they do not need to other members who might get more use out of it.

Reverse table topics

Idea:

This idea was partly inspired by the idea of the backwards meeting. During the table topics portion of the backwards meeting, the table topics speakers all provide table topics speeches without knowing the question that was asked (although they do have a hint of what's to come from the General Evaluator's evaluation) and at the end of each table topics speech, the table topics master comes up with the table topics question that was asked. Rarely does the table topics master have a chance to be creative during table topics (yes, they do have a chance to be creative with table topics themselves) and this gives them the opportunity to turn normal answers into funny situations through the questions asked.

Equipment needed:

None.

What the audience needs to know:

Table topics speakers will not be given a table topics question. Table topics speakers will be selected and then asked to provide a table topics speech of their choosing; however, it should not be simple and straightforward. The table topics speakers will try to 'stump' the table topics master with the answers that they give and the table topics master will try to come up with table topics questions that 'fit' the table topics speeches that were given.

Logistics:

Each table topics speaker will have a moment to think of a crazy or ridiculous table topics speech and when chosen, they will be asked to give that table topics speech (without any prompts or questions from table topics master). At the end of the table topics speech, the table topics master will thank the table topics speaker and provide the table topics question that was answered.

Sample prompts:

None - these are dependent on the creativity and imagination of the table topics master and the table topics speeches given.

Why this idea is great:

This idea is great because the table topics speakers will have fun trying to stump the table topics master and the whole club will have fun hearing what kind of questions the table topics master comes up with.

Mad libs

Idea:

I confess that I was not the person that came up with this idea (and there might even be a small chance that the Toastmaster I saw use this idea was not the first to come up with this idea either). For those of you that do not know what Mad Libs are, you have sentences with specific words missing (e.g., nouns, names, verbs). In pairs, with one person writing and the other person coming up with nouns, adjectives, verbs, etc., the person writing asks the other person for words to fill in the sentences and then fills them into the blank spots. At the end, the person writing will read out the story with all the different nouns, adjectives, verbs that the other person came up with.

For example:

Name: Jack
Verb: Jumping
Adjective: Spicy
Noun: Pancake

Jack was outside jumping because of the spicy pancake. Note that blank spots (I.e., the underlined words) will usually have "Name" or "Verb" underneath them so that the person writing knows what kind of word to ask for.

Equipment needed:

Some slight preparation is needed to print out the mad libs. You do not need to come up with your own mad libs as there are many different stories you can borrow online.

What the audience needs to know:

The table topics master will be conducting 'mad libs' with the whole audience. After filling in all the blanks in the story, the table topics master will choose a table topics speaker to read through the mad libs and make sense of the 'story'.

Logistics:

No special processes are required for this table topics.

Sample prompts:

Google mad libs or you can find printable versions of mad libs on madglibs.com.

Why this idea is great:

I always enjoy table topics where the table topics speakers have to justify a random or ridiculous phrase because it can really push people's creativity to their limits.

The brainstorming session

Idea:

This can be a fantastic idea for business-oriented clubs OR you can change the theme so that it will benefit your club instead (e.g., Getting 40 guests to visit the club in the fiscal year, Membership drive, Marketing campaign).

Equipment needed:

The table topics master will have to prepare for a focused discussion on the topic at hand. They should be open to any idea that any member suggests and encourage constructive debate as opposed to destructive comments.

What the audience needs to know:

The table topics master has a singular goal in mind and each table topics speaker will be sharing an idea to further that goal. The audience should be listening to the table topics speakers so that they can participate and add to the discussion.

Logistics:

The table topics master will first state the goal of the exercise, e.g., "Our goal is to start a business" or "Our goal is to get 40 guests to visit the club". The table topics master will provide a minute so that people can think about the topic and then ask the table topics speakers to speak on the goal.

Sample prompts:

- Why is this goal important?
- What should we focus on (to start a business or to get 40 guests)?
- Who are we targeting? Who are our ideal customers?
- Where are these ideal customers? What is the best way to reach them?
- What is one action that a member can take today to help us with that goal?
- Do we need additional money? Is this something worthwhile to spend money on?
- How do we market this idea? What are different ways to market our idea to let our customers know?
- Are there ways of marketing that you have seen outside of Toastmasters that can be used? How could it be applied to this situation?

Why this idea is great:

Sometimes, the club recognizes that change is needed but often times, it is one or two club executives who need to lead the change and it can be tough if the members are not on board. This idea can help the club executives bring about change because the members will not only have a say in the action plan but will feel that they have more buy-in to the goal.

Debate

Idea:

The debate is a fantastic way of pushing people out of their comfort zones and getting members to think critically about forming logical arguments and rebutting an imaginary opposition.

Equipment needed:

The table topics master will prepare a debate topic that does not necessarily have a correct answer. Generally, if there are recent and relevant news worthy items, these make good topics for debates (e.g., at the time of this writing, Uber is a hot topic - some say that it is a fantastic service while others may think that it is not safe or that it takes away work from taxi drivers).

What the audience needs to know:

The table topics master will act as the facilitator to help guide and walk members through the debate. The members will be split in half into two groups with one group speaking for the topic and the other group speaking against the topic. For example, if the topic is on whether or not the Canadian government should have private planes, one group will speak on why the Canadian government should have private planes and the other group will speak on why the Canadian government should not have private planes.

Logistics:

The table topics master will act as the facilitator and will remain impartial to the debate. Each debater will have the length of a table topic speech to form an argument against any previous arguments and / or to form a new argument. The first debater will only be forming new argument(s) in their table topics speech. At the very end, a member of each group will summarize the arguments in a conclusive speech.

Note that it is important to stress that this is an open debate and that no attacks on people or their character should be encouraged. Any argument is a good argument (I.e., all members should be encouraged to speak).

Sample prompts:

Try to choose topics that do not need a lot of specialized knowledge and that are relevant to your club.

- Should Uber be allowed to displace taxi drivers?
- Should we ban animal testing?
- Does reality television do more harm than good?
- Should we raise the legal driving age to 18?
- Should we ban boxing?

- Should we ban beauty contests?
- Should we lower the drinking age?
- Is downloading music without permission morally equivalent to theft?

Other debate topics can be found by googling "sample debate topics".

Why this idea is great:

Of all the table topic ideas I have ever participated in, this table topic is the one that for some reason makes me the most uncomfortable. Maybe it is because I need a lot of time to craft arguments or maybe because there is no 'right' answer but I can say that I have thoroughly enjoyed and been pushed to my limits every time I have participated in a table topics debate. Members will get the opportunity to practice their active listening and their critical thinking skills.

Film dub

Idea:

As you can probably tell, I am a huge fan of improv and try to find ways to incorporate improv games into table topics as much as possible. This table topics is based on an improv game of the same name. The idea is to show a video clip of people speaking, but to mute the dialogue and have table topics speakers replace or 'dub' the dialogue with their own dialogue.

Equipment needed:

This table topics will need a projector, a laptop and several video clips that you can play for table topics (you can find these on any video site such as YouTube or Vimeo).

Note that the table topics master should watch the clips beforehand to make sure that there are enough table topics speakers for the characters in the clip.

What the audience needs to know:

The table topics master will select several table topics speakers to be the 'speakers' for the clips. Each table topics speaker will be assigned to speak on behalf of a specific character in the clip (e.g., if a man and a woman are talking, one table topics speaker will create the dialogue for the man and the other table topics speaker will create the dialogue for the woman).

Logistics:

Once the table topics speakers have been assigned their characters in the video clip, the table topics master will play the clip. The table topics speech will be to create dialogue whenever the characters in the video speak (I.e., when one or the other character speaks, the table topics speakers will supply the dialogue).

Although there is no hard requirement for the dialogue to make sense, it should make sense as much as possible.

If there are more than three characters in the clip, ask three table topics speakers to dub the clip with the third table topic speaker dubbing the third character and any other additional characters as needed.

Sample prompts:

Try to choose videos or clips that are not mainstream (I.e., choosing a Friend's clip would probably not be the best choice because dubbing something familiar to the members will bias them towards certain topics in the dubbing.

Clips of scenes about 1 - 3 minutes in length would be ideal.

- Bonanza
- I dream of Jeannie
- Fresh Prince of Bel Air
- Days of our lives
- X files
- Full House

Why this idea is great:

The table topics speakers will require a keen eye to notice the body language of the characters in the video clip and how they are interacting with others or their environment or themselves in the clip. Table topics speakers do not need to be funny - the humour comes naturally as a result of the dubbing.

Trailer club

Idea:

A similar idea to the film dub except instead of dubbing a video clip, table topics speakers will dub a trailer and describe the preview of a movie that they have hopefully not seen or know about.

Equipment needed:

This table topics will need a projector, a laptop and several movie trailers that you can play for table topics.

The table topics master does not need to watch the trailers beforehand although it might be a nice way to transition between table topics by talking about what the film trailer actually described.

What the audience needs to know:

The table topics master will select a table topics speaker to dub the trailer for an unknown film.

Logistics:

The table topics speaker will dub a film trailer. When dubbing the film trailer, it is important to remember what any good film trailer contains: it usually contains a protagonist, an antagonist, a specific problem and a cliff-hanger so that people want to watch the movie in theatres.

Sample prompts:

Try to choose films that are not mainstream. If you google the top 100 movie list and show clips of films that were made before the 1950s (please adjust this depending on your club), you should have a list of films that most likely very few people in the room have watched.

Why this idea is great:

Again, it is important to stress that humour is not needed and should not be forced. The table topics speaker has a lot of room for creativity and can take the film in any way (even if the video seems to be going one way such as a romantic comedy). This can also be a great table topics theme for members that are film buffs.

Grab bag

Idea:

Props are a good way of generating table topics and this table topic capitalizes on props as a way to seed topics for the table topics session.

Equipment needed:

The table topics master should prepare a number of props (small tools such as nail clippers, elastic bands, slippers, lemons, etc.) to bring to the meeting.

What the audience needs to know:

The table topics master will announce a goal for the club (e.g., reach 30 active members or to help all new members achieve their competent communicator) and will ask each table topics speaker to share their ideas on how to support that goal, with the prop that they choose from the grab bag.

Logistics:

The table topics speaker, once selected, will grab a prop from the grab bag and will have to incorporate the prop in their speech in some way.

Sample prompts:

- Reach 30 active members
- Introduce the club to 50 guests
- Reach 10 / 10 points on the DCP plan
- Encourage more fun meetings
- Win speech contests
- Create a unique spirit within the club

Why this idea is great:

As the saying goes, one man's garbage is another man's treasure and you never know what a prop might do to influence a table topics speech or to generate innovative and novel ideas that might inspire other members.

The crime scene

Idea:

This table topics idea was inspired by the movie Rashomon, where a story can change based on the perspectives of other characters in the same scene.

Equipment needed:

No special equipment is needed.

What the audience needs to know:

The table topics master, as the detective, will announce that a crime has been committed (e.g., a member that is absent from the meeting has been kidnapped). He will then 'interview' other members of the club to hear where and when they last saw the member. The table topics master can 'guide' the story by adding transition comments or asking leading questions.

For example, if the first table topic speaker saw that the kidnapped member was last seen with Dave, the table topics master can then ask a member what Dave's motive(s) could be in kidnapping the member.

Table topics speeches can be completely made up.

Logistics:

The table topics master will outline the background of the story and will ask various 'witnesses' about the crime.

Sample prompts:

- Can you describe how you know the victim?
- Tell me about the victim's character, what were they like?
- As the first police officer on the scene, can you describe what it was like?
- Tell me what motives might there be in committing this crime?
- Who do you think could have committed this crime?
- You were the last person to see the victim, what were they up to and why?
- Do you think that the victim was up to anything suspicious? Why or why not?

Other questions may come up during the table topics session.

Why this idea is great:

Since the table topics speeches can be completely made up, it only takes one person to come up with a ridiculous table topics speech in order for others to follow along in the fun. It can also help to describe a fairly ridiculous crime "Bob was caught stealing chocolate cookies from the kitchen" or "Jeff was kidnapped and a ransom note was asked for $49.99".

Analogies

Idea:

I am a huge fan of metaphors and similes, especially in speeches and I wanted to see what creative associations people come up with when put on the spot.

Equipment needed:

No special equipment is needed.

What the audience needs to know:

The table topics master will decide on a theme (such as Toastmasters) and then provide random nouns. The table topics speakers will then have to speak on why the theme is like the noun (e.g., Why is Toastmasters like a purse?).

Logistics:

No special logistics are required for this table topics idea.

Sample prompts:

Themes

- Toastmasters
- Theme of the day
- Leadership
- Communication
- Friendship
- Teamwork
- Discipline

Nouns

- Purse
- Shoe
- Slow cooker
- Bed
- Computer
- Toothbrush
- Book
- Pants
- Car
- Loan

Why this idea is great:

I have talked a lot about how there can be creativity within boundaries and constraints and this can be a great way of stimulating creative table topics and word associations. I can also see this table topic idea being naturally funny for many clubs as speakers try to come up with ways that two things that are not normally put in the same sentence, are related.

Idioms

Idea:

Being someone born outside of Canada, I have always found it interesting to hear people use different idioms or phrases that do not literally mean what the phrase is. For example, "a rolling stone gathers no moss" or "you can kill two birds with one stone".

Equipment needed:

No special equipment is needed.

What the audience needs to know:

The table topics master will describe an idiom that is not very well known and will ask a table topics speaker to define the idiom. At the end of the table topics speech, the table topics master can provide the actual definition of the idiom.

Logistics:

No special logistics are required for this table topics idea.

Sample prompts:

- Do a Devon Loch (suddenly fail when everybody expects them to succeed)
- Bob's your uncle (everything is alright)
- Do a runner (leaves a place in a hurry to avoid paying for something)
- Enough to cobble dogs with (a surplus of anything)
- Fall off the back of a lorry (you acquired something that was probably stolen)
- Hairy at the heel (refers to someone who is ill-bred, dangerous or untrustworthy)
- Cat's arse (the facial expression adopted by a scorned woman)
- For donkey's years (do something for a long time without much to show for it)
- To let a frog out of your mouth (say the wrong thing)
- To have a wide face (you are very social and people enjoy having you as company)
- Into the mouth of a wolf (tell someone good luck)
- A cat's jump (a short distance away)
- I sense owls in the moss (find or see something suspicious)
- To feed the donkey sponge cake (you are treating someone well that does not need or deserve your good treatment)
- Catching the fish (nod off or fall asleep)
- To ride as a hare (travel anywhere without a ticket)
- Running while pissing (to do something only to half of your ability)
- To have the mid-day demon (someone having a midlife crisis)
- Not my circus, not my monkeys (it is not my problem)
- Flat out like a lizard drinking (someone is very busy)
- To give someone pumpkins (reject somebody)

- To have a stick in your ear (purposely not listening)
- 50 steps are similar to 100 steps (six of one, half a dozen of the other)
- The hen sees the snake's feet and the snake sees the hen's boobs (two people know each other's secrets)
- Go pick mushrooms (go away / leave me alone)

More can be found by searching for "idioms from other cultures" - this can be a good way of keeping the idioms strange and bizarre for at least most of the members of your club.

Why this idea is great:

The great thing about Toastmasters is that people from all backgrounds and ethnicities come together to form a club; no club will have the same members and as a result, no club will have the same experience or feel. This table topic explores that diversity and can be a great way of getting other members to bond with one another through their backgrounds.

Music clips

Idea:

Almost everyone listens to music and everyone listens to music for a particular reason. This table topic explores the memories that people associate with different types of music.

Equipment needed:

Something to play music is needed (could be a phone and then a speaker, could be a phone that is turned up, could be a laptop, etc.)

What the audience needs to know:

The table topics master will play a clip of music that can be from any genre and the table topics speaker will tell the audience about the first thing or memory they thought of when they listened to that clip of music. They can also talk about the artist that plays or sings the music, the genre of music and whether they like it or any other topic related to the song.

Logistics:

No special logistics are required for this table topics idea.

Sample prompts:

- You can use music from your personal collection or use a music streaming service such as rdio or slacker radio or even just search up clips from YouTube. Try a few of these genres:

  - Country
  - Rap
  - EDM
  - R&B
  - Classical
  - Folk music
  - Instrumental
  - House

The more bizarre and eccentric the genre, the better. You can also use mainstream music but I would recommend playing mainstream music for guests or first-timers.

Why this idea is great:

Table topics speakers can take the idea in different ways but music is something that almost everyone listens to and can identify with so this table topic can invoke a lot of great table topic speeches and help members learn more about each other and the type of music they listen to.

Random YouTube videos

Idea:

A picture tells a thousand words and therefore a video tells... a million words?

Equipment needed:

A laptop or a computer that can project to a screen or television.

What the audience needs to know:

The table topics master will play a random video clip and the table topics speaker will talk about the first thing they think of when they watch the clip.

Logistics:

No special logistics are required for this table topics idea; however, if the video clip is longer than a minute, the table topics master will stop the clip.

Sample prompts:

The more bizarre the video, the better but you can google "random YouTube videos" and just play clips off of the site.

- http://randomyoutube.net/watch#
- http://ytroulette.com/?i=19&c=0

Why this idea is great:

Just like the music clips table topics idea, the table topics speakers can take the speech many different ways that may only be tangentially related to the video. This table topics idea is also a great way to see what kind of YouTube videos exist on the internet.

Quotes from a book

Idea:

A great way to explore the 'nuggets' of a book.

Equipment needed:

Any book.

What the audience needs to know:

The table topics master will read a small passage from a book - it can be a quote or it can be a small paragraph. The table topics speakers will talk about what they think of the quote or what story it inspires them to remember.

Logistics:

No special logistics are required for this table topics idea.

Sample prompts:

- Take any book that you own (or borrow a book from work / friends) and read a sample quote from the book. Generally, there are lots of great quotes at the end of a chapter (for fiction and non-fiction books) or anything that is highlighted in some way in the book (bold, underlined, and italicized).

Why this idea is great:

Whenever we read a book, we generally do not remember everything from a book but more of the 'nuggets' of the book. This table topics idea can be a great way of exploring the 'nuggets' of the book without reading the whole book word for word.

Start-up names

Idea:

A great way to be creative with names in general.

Equipment needed:

No special equipment needed.

What the audience needs to know:

The table topics master will provide a name of a start-up (the start-up can be real or made up). Each table topics speaker will then develop a short business plan of the start-up based on the name of the start-up. The table topics speaker will talk about the product, the markets that they play in, the customers they are looking for and how they plan on marketing the product to customers.

Logistics:

No special logistics are required for this table topics idea.

Sample prompts:

- elexa
- movza
- izbe
- azig
- coolidea
- sandsome
- butling
- churchew
- cousness
- elegency
- quishes
- unddad

Find more start-up names through random start-up name generators online:

- http://www.naminum.com/
- http://www.namemesh.com/company-name-generator
- http://shobia.com/namebird

Why this idea is great:

You can see that some of the prompts are not related to anything in general but you can choose prompts that actually mean something in English to help the table topics speakers. For a business-focused club, this can also be a great way of stimulating business skills in a safe environment.

Apps

Idea:

A great way to learn more about members through the technology that they use.

Equipment needed:

The audience should bring smartphones or tablets to the meeting if they own one.

What the audience needs to know:

The table topics master will look through any smartphones or tablets and name an app on the phone that people may not have heard of. They will then ask a table topics speaker (not the same owner of the phone) to talk about the app, describe what it does and why everybody should be using it.

Logistics:

You may need to ask the audience if they are okay with you digging through their phones and looking at the apps that they use. If not, that is okay - make sure to have a few extra apps on your phone that you can ask the audience about.

Sample prompts:

- PETAL (Pattern Enhancement Tool for Assisting Landmine Sensing)
- Blower
- Annoy-a-teen
- iBlackout
- Cubecheater
- Fake Call
- Sleep Sheep
- Geico Brostache
- Game for Cats

Find more apps by asking Toastmasters whether you can look through their phones for apps.

Why this idea is great:

If the other person is okay with it, I've found that a great way of learning more about someone and finding common interests is to look through their home screen to see how they use their smartphone and what they use it for. Since almost everyone these days have smartphones, you can learn more about some bizarre apps and learn more about other members.

Apples to apples

Idea:

A fantastic way to show that creativity can be as simple as matching together adjectives and nouns.

Equipment needed:

None needed but if someone has the board game "Apples to Apples", that would help out table topics. Alternatively, the table topics master can write out different index cards with a noun on each card and an adjective on each card (e.g., 10 cards with one noun each and 10 cards with one adjective each).

What the audience needs to know:

The table topics speaker will pick one card from the nouns and one card from the adjectives and their speech will be about why the noun is the adjective. For example, if the adjective was "fascinating" and the noun was "heels" then the table topics speaker will talk about why heels are fascinating. The table topics speaker can take the topic in many different directions as long as they answer the main question of why heels are fascinating (e.g., women who wear heels are fascinating, heels are fascinating because they are uncomfortable yet women still wear them).

Logistics:

The table topics master will fan out two decks of cards - one with only nouns and one with only adjectives. The table topics speaker will choose one card from each deck.

Sample prompts:

Nouns:
- Heels
- Books
- Scissors
- Toilet paper
- Knives
- Jackets
- Smartphones
- Cars
- Flashlights
- A's (the letter)
- Angels
- Christmas Trees
- Alcohol sanitizer
- Cups
- Humans

- Toastmasters

Adjectives:
- Sexy
- Gross
- Educational
- Lovely
- Weird
- Obscure
- Ridiculous
- Romantic
- Flirtatious
- Grotesque
- Horrible
- Kind
- Generous

Feel free to use other nouns or adjectives that are specific to your club.

Why this idea is great:

If you take a look at the list of adjectives and nouns, you can see that the table topics speech is challenging yet can be taken in a lot of different directions which helps to make it easier for table topics speakers. Also, depending on the noun and adjective, this can be quite humorous as you hear table topics speakers try to explain their way out of the noun and adjective.

Dance moves

Idea:

A fun way of incorporating body language and movement into table topics.

Equipment needed:

No equipment needed although if you want to make it extra fun, you can play some music using a smartphone or laptop while table topics speakers are dancing.

What the audience needs to know:

The table topics master will provide different prompts for dance moves and the table topics speaker will have to dance out the moves and describe how the dance moves came about.

Logistics:

No special logistics are required for this table topics idea.

Sample prompts:

- The lonely cat
- The gigantic elephant
- The broken down car
- The energetic windmill
- The silent blender
- The leaky faucet
- The gurgling toilet
- The creepy porch swing
- The funky showerhead
- The inconsistent baseball swing
- The misty humidifier
- The clicking keyboard
- The surprise punch

You can also use their names. For example, the "Wang Yip" - what would that dance move look like?

Why this idea is great:

The prompts have a huge potential for fun and creativity and I purposely chose prompts which already have specific motions that we are used to so that it is easier for table topics speakers to be inspired to do certain dance moves (e.g., a porch swing dance move could be simply bracing yourself on two tables and then swinging your legs back and forth).

Tell us something we do not know

Idea:

I enjoy listening to podcasts and one of my favourite podcasts is The Dinner Party Download. In the podcast, one of their two main questions is: "Tell us something we do not know and this can be about yourself or the world". I've started to use the same question myself when meeting new people and I thought this would be a great table topics question to ask everyone.

Equipment needed:

No equipment needed.

What the audience needs to know:

The table topics master will ask everyone the same question: "Tell us something we do not know and this can be something about yourself or a random fact in the world".

Logistics:

No special logistics are required for this table topics idea.

Sample prompts:

No sample prompts as the question for all table topics speakers will be the same.

Why this idea is great:

This is a nice and easy table topics question that is great for meetings with a lot of guests - not only will members be prepared for the table topics speech (because they already know the question) but you will get to learn something about the guests as well and it can be quite surprising what Toastmasters reveal about themselves or the world around them (which can tell you a lot about what they like doing with their time).

Random facts

Idea:

I always like learning new facts, even if they may not be all that useful to my work or life. On my android phone, I have an app called "Daily Curiosity" which shares 5 new, random facts every day. Even better than learning random facts is learning the connection between a random fact to something that we can actually use in our lives and that is what this table topic captures.

Equipment needed:

No equipment needed.

What the audience needs to know:

The table topics master will provide everyone with two random facts and just like examining the six degrees of Kevin Bacon, the table topics speaker will explore how the two random facts are connected by linking them to things that they know.

Logistics:

No special logistics are required for this table topics idea.

Sample prompts:

- G-LOC stands for G-induced loss of consciousness - it occurs when gravitational forces drain blood away from the brain, and most often affects pilots and astronauts
- The zipper was originally called the "clasp locker" - the original design used a series of hooks and eye instead of interlocking teeth
- A limnic eruption causes a lake to "explode" and release a deadly cloud of carbon dioxide. The 1986 limnic eruption of Lake Nyos asphyxiated around 1,700 people
- Eleanor Roosevelt earned 35 honorary degrees while her husband, President Franklin D. Roosevelt only received 31
- Your iris is more unique than your fingerprint
- The first contact lenses were made of glasses and were 8 - 15 mm thick
- You don't cry tears in space - they become liquid balls stuck on your face
- Banging your head against a wall burns 150 calories an hour
- When hippos are upset, their sweat turns red
- May 29th is officially "Put a Pillow on your Fridge Day"
- Heart attacks are more likely to happen on a Monday
- A toaster uses almost half as much energy as a full-sized oven
- If you leave everything to the last minute, it will only take a minute
- The first alarm clock could only ring at 4 am
- Each year, there are more than 40,000 toilet related injuries in the United States
- The most common name in the world is Mohammed
- The most money ever paid for a cow in an auction was $1.3 million

- The elephant is the only animal with 4 knees
- The elephant is the only mammal that cannot jump
- You burn more calories sleeping than you do watching TV

Remember that you will need at least twice as many random facts as table topics speakers you want to ask and you can find more random facts by using the app I previously mentioned or by googling "random facts". Alternatively, you can make table topics easier by asking for the history of the fact or why this is important to us in everyday lives.

Why this idea is great:

Not only do you learn something new, this is a table topic that can help participants practice connecting different, disparate ideas together and hone their critical thinking skills.

The instruction manual

Idea:

Whenever I meet someone new, I always take it as an opportunity to learn something about the world that I did not know before. This is what I tried to capture in this table topic.

Equipment needed:

No equipment needed.

What the audience needs to know:

The table topics master will ask everyone to teach them something that they did not know before. This table topic will also teach them how to organize and structure their speech because they will have to provide a set of instructions on how to do something. Each table topics speech will be a set of instructions on how to do something in particular.

Logistics:

No special logistics are required for this table topics idea.

Sample prompts:

You can ask each table topics speaker to teach them something that they think very few people know or you can provide them with a prompt on something ridiculous. It might even be best to mix it up and sometimes provide them with a prompt and then sometimes ask them to teach the audience something that very few people know about.

- How to defuse a bomb
- How to deliver a baby
- How to have a happy family
- How to find and cook snails
- How to keep your house clean
- How to fix your yacht
- How to be a superhero
- How to fly a plane
- How to be a CEO

These are just a few prompts that can be used. The best prompts are those without specific answers, or rather, specific right answers because then the table topics speakers can take the speech anywhere they would like.

Why this idea is great:

Shifting between the known (what table topics speakers know already) and the unknown (the prompts), this can be a great way of learning something new both in terms of the table topic, but also the member's interests. Perhaps they know exactly how to defuse a bomb or how to fix a yacht. In that case, they will be able to teach the audience something new and it will definitely be a source of small talk later.

Before and after

Idea:

This idea was inspired by a game on Wheel of Fortune called "Before and After". Phrases are linked together and table topics speakers must discover the connection between the two phrases.

Equipment needed:

No equipment needed.

What the audience needs to know:

The table topics master will ask the audience a question about the before and after phrase. Once the audience guesses the phrase, the table topics master will ask one table topics speaker to

Logistics:

No special logistics are required for this table topics idea.

Sample prompts:

Each prompt comes with a question about the phrase.
- A Blast from the Past, Present and Future (What's the connection between a Brendan Fraser and Alicia Silverstone movie and a description of all time periods?)
- A Hole in One Way Ticket (What's the connection between a great golf shot and travel to Mars?)
- Adam's Apple of My Eye (What's the connection between a body part named after a man and someone that you cherish?)
- Add Fuel to the Fire Extinguisher (What's the connection between causing a situation to become more intense and a device to get rid of flames?)
- America's Next Top Model Train Set (What's the connection between a runway model show and locomotive toys that you might get as a hobby?)
- American Express Yourself (What's the connection between a brand of credit cards and individuality?)
- Ceiling Fan Club (What's the connection between an air circulator inside the home and a group of people dedicated to a celebrity?)
- Curiousity Killed the Cat Burglar (What's the connection between how a feline dies and a petty robber?)
- Fame & Fortune Cookie (What's the connection between what all movie stars seek and a Chinese dessert?)
- Go Ahead Make My Day Care Center (What's the connection between a Clint Eastwood famous line and a place that takes care of young kids?)

These are just a few prompts that can be used. The best prompts are those without specific answers, or rather, specific right answers because then the table topics speakers can take the speech anywhere they would like.

Why this idea is great:

I like that this table topic quizzes the audience first, before giving them a table topic to answer. Often times, once the audience has made the connection, there will be some humour in the juxtaposition of the two phrases.

Tim Ferriss questions

Idea:

I am a huge fan of Tim Ferriss and his podcast that interviews some of the best teachers in the world and dives into the things that they do that make them the best. These questions are all from his podcast and can be used to explore some of the unique things

Equipment needed:

No equipment needed.

What the audience needs to know:

The table topics master will ask everyone a random question on their productivity and the habits or activities that help them be the best.

Logistics:

No special logistics are required for this table topics idea.

Sample prompts:

Most questions are from the Timothy Ferriss podcast.

- What is the best under $100 purchase that you have made in the past year that has significantly improved the quality of your life?
- What does the first 90 minutes of your day look like? When do you wake up? What do you do?
- If we asked your friends and family what you are the best at, what would they say and why?
- If you had a billboard that you could place anywhere, what would you put on it and where would you put it?
- What software / apps do you use that help you with your productivity?
- What is something mind blowing that you have seen recently in terms of work hacks?
- What books have you gifted the most to other people?
- What books, podcasts, audiobooks, etc. have you recently read or listened to that have really helped you become more productive?
- What are the most common mistakes in your profession?
- Who are the people that you follow or learn from?

Why this idea is great:

Not only can this be a great table topic to dive into some things that people do that make them amazing but this can also be a really great way of getting to know someone new.

Free advertisements

Idea:

There is nothing like a good advertisement that can really help shape your opinions about a brand or a product and unconsciously, whether we like it or not, advertisements are all around us and do affect us, even if we think that they don't. Making a good advertisement is tough though and I wanted to explore that process with table topics speakers.

Equipment needed:

A list of local businesses in your city / country that few people know anything about.

What the audience needs to know:

The table topics master will ask table topics speakers to come up with a short 1 - 2 minute advertisement for the business that they have found. If the business is not immediately obvious, the table topics master will describe what the business does.

It may be important to understand the components of a good advertisement:

- Features of the product or service
- Benefits
- Urgency
- Offer (why does the customer need the service or product)

Logistics:

No special logistics are required for this table topics idea.

Sample prompts:

The yellow pages online is a great resource for finding local businesses. I took a look through some of the businesses and found a few that I would use for table topics (feel free to use these or find your own):

- Cougar Paint and Collision Inc.
- Key Agventures (Farm Equipment, Contractor's Equipment Service and Supplies)
- Pearson's Berry Farm and Homestyle Beverages (Fruit and Berry Farm and Shipping)
- JT's Bar and Grill
- Buffalo Valley (Buffalo meat butcher shop)
- Easyfix Appliance (Repair service)
- Lucid Landscapes Limited (landscape contractors and designers)
- CMR Recycling and Trucking (Transportation services)
- ABC Weddings
- Prestige Limousine

Why this idea is great:

I enjoy table topics that are fun, challenging and educational and this table topic hits all three. Selling is also an important part of any job no matter where you work or what you do and therefore, practicing selling can be an invaluable skill to move everyone forward in their careers.

Exploring table topics structures

Idea:

As a table topics speaker, one way to prepare for table topics is by understanding the different types of structures that you can use for your speech. This table topics idea pairs simple questions with different speech structures so that table topics speakers can understand and practice the different types of speech structures that can be used. A different speech structure has the ability to make a table topics question easier to answer.

Equipment needed:

No special equipment needed.

What the audience needs to know:

The table topics master will explain a type of speech structure that can be used for table topics and then provide a prompt. They will then ask someone to answer the prompt trying to use the speech structure explained.

Logistics:

No special logistics are required for this table topics idea.

Sample prompts:

Different speech structures that can be used:

- Organized by topics (I have 3 topics / reasons / aspects / features that I want to share today)
- Organized chronologically (i.e., by time or by talking about how the topic has changed from the past, to present to the future)
- Organized spatially (i.e., by geography or physical structure)
- Organized by cause and effect (what was the cause of the subject and what was the effect?)
- Organized by pros and cons (you can take one side of an argument or your speech could explore both the pros and cons and leave it open for the audience)
- Organized by a trick (e.g., alliteration, rhyme, mnemonic, the three C's of interviewing or the four B's of taking care of a child)
- Organized by problem and then solutions (i.e., you introduce a problem in your speech and explore the various solutions that can solve the problem)

Different prompts:

- Communication
- Leadership
- Chores
- Technology

- Public Speaking
- Shoes
- Food
- Work
- Money

Why this idea is great:

Although the prompts can be easy, it is not as easy to try to fit your speech into a specific structure; however, as this is practice for future table topics speeches, you are now allowed to use any of the speech structures explained to your advantage when explaining a table topic. Talking about communication and how it has changed from the past to the present to the future can be easier than talking about the pros and cons of communication.

Shakespeare quotes

Idea:

The great poet and playwright has a prolific amount of creative works that has generated discussion. Why not use some of those choice quotes for table topics?

Equipment needed:

The table topics master should research quotes from Shakespeare (about 10 - 15) before table topics.

What the audience needs to know:

The table topics master will ask each table topics speaker to comment on the Shakespeare quote.

Logistics:

No special logistics are required for this table topics idea.

Sample prompts:

Here are a few quotes that I believe make for good table topics speeches:

- "There is nothing either good or bad, but thinking makes it so" - Hamlet in Hamlet
- "Action is eloquence" - Volumnia in Coriolanus
- "Come what come may, time and the hour runs through the roughest day" - Macbeth in Macbeth
- "If love be blind, it best agrees with night" - Juliet in Romeo and Juliet
- "All that glisters is not gold" - Prince of Morocco In The Merchant of Venice
- "Love looks not with the eyes but with the mind" - Helena in A Midsummer Night's Dream
- "The course of true love never did run smooth" - A Midsummer Night's Dream
- "Brevity is the soul of wit" - Hamlet
- "One may smile, and smile, and be a villain" - Hamlet
- "Some are born great, others achieve greatness" - Twelfth Night
- "If we are true to ourselves, we cannot be false to anyone" - Hamlet
- "Love is merely a madness" - As You Like It

Why this idea is great:

I cannot honestly say that I like Shakespeare plays, but I do believe that there is wisdom in his plays and I have to admire his craft. Table topics can also be made more challenging by choosing different quotes that do not have an obvious implication or meaning (though if this is your first time introducing Shakespeare in table topics, you may want to stay with some of the easier quotes for now).

Favourites

Idea:

A great way of generating discussions is to ask for people's opinions on their favourite things. I love asking these types of questions to people I've just met because it helps me learn something new and helps me find things that I have in common with that person.

Equipment needed:

No special equipment is needed.

What the audience needs to know:

The table topics master will ask each table topics speaker to comment on their favourite thing (thing to be determined by the table topics master).

Logistics:

No special logistics are required for this table topics idea.

Sample prompts:

- What is your favourite restaurant?
- What is your favourite movie?
- What is your favourite music album / song?
- What is your favourite way of traveling?
- What is your favourite book?
- What is your favourite way to spend free time?
- What is your favourite place to take a visitor?
- What is your favourite comfort food?
- What is your favourite way of relaxing?
- What is your favourite piece of clothing?

Why this idea is great:

This is a relatively easy table topics that will help members get to know one another and for members to connect with guests through their answers.

Excuses

Idea:

We all know how lame and cheesy excuses can be, but what if we are the ones who have to come up with the excuses? What would we come up with?

Equipment needed:

No special equipment is needed.

What the audience needs to know:

The table topics master will put each table topics speaker into an uncomfortable situation that they have to explain themselves out of.

Logistics:

No special logistics are required for this table topics idea.

Sample prompts:

- Your boss comes by your desk and finds that you were sleeping. Explain yourself!
- You are late to the job interview. Explain yourself!
- While you are volunteering, you get into a fight with another volunteer. Explain yourself!
- At school, your homework is due and you have not completed it. Explain yourself!
- You have lost the keys to your house and decide to break a window to get in; however, the police catch you in the act. Explain yourself!
- You are a policeman and as you make an arrest, you seemed to have lost your police badge. Explain yourself!
- An angel investor has given you one million dollars to invest in your business idea, but at the end of the year, you have not made any progress. Explain yourself!
- You are out at a romantic dinner with your spouse and are terribly hungry. When the entrees arrive, your spouse goes to the washroom and when they come back, both entrees have been devoured. Explain yourself!
- While attending a funeral, you are bored and start to play with your smartphone; however, you are caught by the grieving family. Explain yourself!
- While watching a movie at a theatre, your phone rings loudly in the middle of a critical scene. Everyone is angry at you. Explain yourself!
- After a long day at work, you come home to realize that you forgot to pick up your partner from the airport! Running outside, you see your partner arriving in a taxi. Explain yourself!

Why this idea is great:

Excuses are always fun to hear and these may give the members ideas on how to explain themselves out of situations in the future.

Lies

Idea:

This is similar to Excuses, except table topics speakers are put into a situation in which they have to lie (even if everything seems true).

Equipment needed:

No special equipment is needed.

What the audience needs to know:

The table topics master will put each table topics speaker into a situation in which they have to lie. Each table topics speaker will provide a back story as to how this situation came to be.

Logistics:

No special logistics are required for this table topics idea.

Sample prompts:

- You are a Toastmaster, aren't you?
- You are a <<that person's job>>, aren't you?
- You are a human, aren't you?
- You are <<person's ethnicity>>, aren't you?
- You do need water to survive, don't you?
- You breathe air, don't you?
- You need money to survive, don't you?
- You're wearing shoes, aren't you?
- You're wearing underwear, aren't you?
- You have hair on your head, don't you?

Why this idea is great:

There's an incredible amount of freedom that comes from not having to tell the truth and I wanted table topics speakers to free themselves by saying anything they want without having to justify that it is true or worry about the logistics of anything.

Never have I ever

Idea:

There's a fun game that Ellen DeGeneres plays with her guests whenever a big movie comes out - it's called "Never have I ever" and the guests have to answer truthfully on whether or not they have done something.

Equipment needed:

Big cards / print outs for everyone in the audience is needed. On one side of the print out are the words "I have" and the other side "I have never".

What the audience needs to know:

The table topics master will ask a series of questions and then look to the audience to see who has done it and who has not done it. The table topics question will be dependent on the table topics master. As any good table topics master knows, they need to identify who has big speaking roles and choose the appropriate people. Therefore, they can ask the appropriate people based on the answers (e.g., if someone says they have seen a ghost, the table topics master might ask that person to tell the audience the story).

Logistics:

No special logistics are required for this table topics idea.

Sample prompts:

- Never ever have I ever been to a nude beach
- Never ever have I ever been on a bad date
- Never ever have I been arrested
- Never ever have I gotten a tattoo
- Never ever have I lied in Toastmasters
- Never ever have I lied to my boss
- Never ever have I stolen something from work
- Never ever have I said a baby was cute when it was obviously ugly
- Never ever have I seen a ghost
- Never ever have I ever forgotten the name of someone I just met
- Never ever have I screamed during a scary movie
- Never ever have I cheated to win a game
- Never ever have I gotten wasted

Why this idea is great:

If everyone in the group is comfortable with it, this can be a great way of breaking the ice and learning about others (as well as the stories behind some of the interesting things they have done).

Topic substitution

Idea:

I saw this idea on YouTube and found it very similar to my press conference idea. The idea is to ask the table topics speaker to leave the room (or put on headphones so that they cannot hear the topic) and to tell the audience that the table topics speaker is talking about one topic. Once the audience knows what the table topics speaker will be speaking about, you will hand the table topics speaker a slip of paper with a different but related topic that they will speak about. This is similar to the press conference idea in the sense that the audience is 'in' on the inside joke while the table topics speaker is not.

Equipment needed:

- Slips of paper with the normal table topics question written or typed on them.
- Headphones and a portable music player (optional)

What the audience needs to know:

The table topics master will ask one table topics speaker to either leave the room or to put on headphones with music playing so that he / she cannot hear what is being said in the room. The table topics master will tell the audience what table topic the speaker will be speaking on (funny table topics). The table topics speaker will then come back to the room or take their headphones off and be provided a slip of paper (normal table topics) to speak on.

Logistics:

If the table topics master has not brought headphones, the Sergeant at Arms can escort table topics speakers just outside the room and the table topics master can whisper the funny table topics to the audience. It may be a better use of time to bring headphones as the table topics speaker can take the headphones on and off quite easily.

Sample prompts:

Note that only normal table topics are provided to table topics speakers. Funny table topics are provided to the audience in secret without the table topics speaker knowing.

- How to write your own obituary (funny table topic)
- How to write a magazine article (normal table topic)

- Father telling his son the birds and the bees speech (funny table topic)
- Telling someone how to open a lock, who has never heard of a lock and key (normal table topic)

- How to be a great partner in a relationship (funny table topic)
- Telling someone how to treat their dog, who has never heard of a dog (normal table topic)

- How to choose a pet (funny table topic)
- Telling someone how to choose a sofa at a store who has never heard of a sofa or any other piece of furniture (normal table topic)

- How to lose weight (funny table topic)
- Telling someone how to get all the toothpaste out of a tube, but they have never heard of toothpaste or seen a tube (normal table topic)

- How to get in shape (funny table topic)
- Telling someone how to get their money's worth at a buffet, who has never heard of a buffet (normal table topic)

- How to get a date (funny table topic)
- Telling someone tips for negotiating, without using the word 'negotiate' (normal table topic)

Why this idea is great:

It's certainly possible that whatever the table topics speaker comes up with for their normal table topic won't necessarily fit into the funny table topic, but the table topics speaker will be genuinely confused as to why the audience may be laughing at seemingly innocuous and innocent statements and the audience will definitely have a great time trying to understand what the table topics speaker is speaking about.

New inventions

Idea:

I am always amazed at the creativity and innovation that happens in the world. Take one look at Kickstarter, and you can see thousands of ideas that make you think "why didn't I think of that?" I wanted to explore some of those crazy ideas by doing something crazy for table topics and asking speakers to justify those crazy ideas.

Equipment needed:

No special equipment is needed.

What the audience needs to know:

The table topics master will provide two random nouns. The table topics speaker is to pretend that they are an inventor and that they have just created one object which is a two-in-one object of the two random nouns. For example, if the table topics master provided "purse" and "shoe", the inventor will talk about their new invention (a purse which is also a shoe). The inventor can talk about what they have named this invention, why they invented it, what problem it solves, who should purchase it, etc.

Logistics:

The table topics master will list out two random prompts (from below or their own) and will then choose the table topics speaker to speak on the topic.

For example: "Our next table topics speaker has just invented a seat belt which is also deodorant. Bob, tell us about your new seat belt and deodorant invention."

Sample prompts:

- Balloon
- White out
- Shirt
- Seat belt
- Wallet
- Flowers
- Key chain
- Magnet
- Candle
- Ketchup bottle
- Pillow
- Clock
- Glasses
- Toothpaste

- Sponge
- Sticky note
- Slippers
- Sketch pad
- Helmet
- TV
- Couch
- Tire swing
- Brown bag
- Socks
- Shampoo
- Picture frame
- Leg warmers
- Deodorant
- Rubber band
- Remote control
- Hair brush

Why this idea is great:

There can be a lot of creativity and humour in combining two seemingly unrelated objects and perhaps some of these table topics speeches will generate actually good ideas.

Thank You

I'd like to express my gratitude for purchasing my e-book. I know you could have picked from dozens of books about public speaking, but you took a chance with me and I greatly appreciate it.

Now I'd like to ask for a small favour. Could you please take a minute or two and leave a review for this book on Amazon?

This feedback will help me continue to write great Kindle books that help you get the results you are looking for.

More Kindle eBooks by Wang

Make Your Speech More Impactful – 10 tips (+ 1 bonus tip) on delivering an impactful speech.

How to Create and Deliver Great Speeches (A Seven Day Approach)

A guide to evaluating speeches – How to prepare, construct and provide impactful evaluations

100+ tips for speakers – Improve your speaking, deliver effective presentations and become more confident in front of an audience

www.ingramcontent.com/pod-product-compliance
Lightning Source LLC
Chambersburg PA
CBHW051328220526

45468CB00004B/1549